Introduction

Hair metal and hair bands have been woefully underrated in the infamous Rock and Roll Hall of Fame. To give these amazing bands and musicians the credit they deserve, we decided to create our own version which celebrates the greatest glam, hair metal and hair bands of all time.

The worst thing about any Hall of Fame is when they oversaturate the membership with inductees that are "borderline" worthy of the establishment. There are more than 300 people in the Major League Baseball Hall of Fame. There are hundreds of artists in the Rock and Roll Hall of Fame. To be honest, in both cases it is just too many and it cheapens the honor of being selected.

So, for our Hall of Fame we wanted to limit it to the "best of the best." If we had to debate for more than thirty seconds on a band, then that band didn't make the cut. Doesn't mean they weren't great. Doesn't mean they didn't put out some fantastic music. It just simply means they weren't the "best of the best."

We used the same criteria here that we used to create the Top 1,000 songs and 350 albums lists for our book: *Soundtrack of Our Youth: History of Hair Metal Music* (available on Amazon). Our top 1,000 list was separated into the top 650 rock songs and top 350 ballads.

Billboard success, touring numbers, iconic nature of the band/music, how good the band was with their respective instruments, as well as several other factors. And again, this isn't a list of our "favorite" bands. If it was, Tora Tora, Junkyard and Dangerous Toys would be sure-fire Hall of Famers!

There are a few bands that you are going to say, "Wait a minute, these guys should definitely be in the Hall of Fame." And we get that. And to be honest, a couple of the bands left out did surprise us at first. But when you look at the numbers, their career totals just didn't add up. And there is one band that made the Hall that surprised us. But their career achievements were too hard to ignore.

So, with that said, here is our list of the greatest Hair Metal / Hair Band / Sleaze Rockers / Arena Rock / Glam bands of all time.

All quotes in this book are taken from interviews we personally conducted with the musicians.

Special thanks to the great **Jamie Cook** for his help editing this book!

Table of Contents
Mt Rushmore
Bon Jovi..................................6
Guns N' Roses.......................13
Def Leppard..........................20
Motley Crue..........................25

Theatre Headliners
Tesla......................................31
Whitesnake...........................34
Skid Row...............................37
L.A. Guns..............................40
Warrant.................................43
Great White..........................46
Dokken..................................49
Ratt.......................................52
Poison...................................55
Kix...58
Cinderella.............................60

Openers
Mr. Big..................................62
White Lion............................63
Winger..................................65
FireHouse..............................66
Slaughter..............................68
Stryper..................................69
Vixen.....................................71
Europe..................................72

The Godfathers
Quiet Riot.............................74
Twisted Sister.......................76
Hanoi Rocks..........................78

Individual Hall of Fame
Jani Lane...............................80
Slash.....................................83
Warren DiMartini..................83
Billy Sheehan........................84
Rod Morgenstein..................84
Axl Rose................................84

Vito Bratta..........................84
Rudy Sarzo..........................84
Mark Mendoza......................85
Tommy Lee..........................85
Don Dokken..........................85
George Lynch......................85
Paul Gilbert........................85
Jimm D'Anda........................85
Akira Takasaki....................85
Blas Elias..........................86
Vik Foxx............................86
Steve Lynch........................86
Greg Chaisson......................86
Jack Russell........................86
David Coverdale..................86
Reb Beach............................86
Jeff Pilson..........................86
Sebastian Bach....................87
Frankie Banali....................87
Eric Martin........................87
Joe Elliott..........................87
Tom Keifer..........................87
Robert Sweet......................87
A.J. Pero............................87
Richie Kotzen 87
Juan Croucier......................88
Ronni Le Tekro....................88
Kyle Kyle............................88
Pepsi Tate..........................88
Mick Brown..........................88
Fred Coury..........................88
Stephen Pearcy....................88
Rick Savage........................89
Dee Snider..........................89
Jesper Binzer......................89
Nikki Sixx..........................89
Rachel Bolan......................89
Lita Ford............................89
Stevie Rachelle....................89

Mt. Rushmore

These are the absolute best bands from the 1981–2019 HM/HB (hair metal/hair band) era. Without question, without a debate. These are the guys that could headline a tour in the 80s, 90s and even sell out arenas today. These bands are the cream of the crop, the four best HM/HBs of the entire era. Any conversation about hair metal has to start and stop with these amazing groups.

Our Hall of Fame is a three–story building. The following four bands occupy the top floor, as well as having their banners hanging on the outside of the building. Floor two are the bands that were A–list openers or that could headline a theatre. Floor three are really solid bands, that have multiple great albums, and were clearly a step above the majority of hair metal bands out there.

It doesn't get any better than these bands.

(Billboard 200 is how they rank albums, Billboard Hot 100 is how they rank individual songs. In the book we will also refer to the 200 as the album chart, and the Hot 100 as the singles chart)

Bon Jovi

Bon Jovi burst on the scene in 1983 and have been rocking sold out stadiums ever since. Bon Jovi and Guns N' Roses are the only bands on the list that can still sell out 50,000 seat venues in 2019.

Bon Jovi has more than 40 songs on our Top 1,000 list, the most of any band. They've also got the second most slow songs in our Top 350 Ballads list. BJ is also easily the most successful Billboard band of the genre. Jon and the boys had 25 songs chart on the Billboard Hot 100, including four number one songs, ten songs in the top ten, and an amazing six albums that reached #1 on the Billboard 200.

Bon Jovi has sold the most albums of any band in our Hall of Fame, barely beating out Guns N' Roses for the top spot. But an incredible 40 million more than the third band on our Mt. Rushmore – Def Leppard.

The song "Runaway" and two pretty solid rock albums that started off Bon Jovi's career. Then all hell broke loose. BJ's next two albums might be the best 1–2 album punch from any band in the genre. *Slippery When Wet* came out in 1986 and inspired thousands of young rockers. *SWW* ended up being the top selling album of the year and spent eight weeks at number one on the Billboard 200 chart. "You Give Love a Bad Name" and "Living on a Prayer" both went to number one on the singles chart.

How do you follow up one of the best–selling albums of all time? For Bon Jovi it was easy. *New Jersey* came out in 1988 and promptly went to number one on Billboard. Again, two singles reached number one ("Bad Medicine" and "I'll Be

There for You"). *New Jersey* featured five songs that charted on the Billboard singles top 10 list, which was a record at the time for a hard rock album. BJ took time off from a grueling worldwide touring schedule to set another rock trend when they went acoustic and played "Livin' On A Prayer" and "Wanted Dead or Alive" at the 1989 MTV Music Awards show.

"Once the second album came out we were all on board," – Danny Vaughn, Tyketto.

Guitar legend Richie Sambora and singer Jon Bon Jovi were both inducted into the Songwriter's Hall of Fame in 2009.

The band is also well known for their charitable acts. Jon runs The Jon Bon Jovi Soul Foundation, which gives aid and assistance to families who have experienced economic woes. The foundation's restaurant JBJ Soul Kitchen allows people to pay what they can afford for their meal. Or, if they have no money, customers can donate their time to cover their meal. The band's drummer Tico Torres runs the Tico Torres Children Foundation, which focuses on children who suffer from hunger, disease, homelessness, neglect, abuse and illness. Sambora has dedicated time/money to numerous well know charities, including those ran by Steve Young and Michael J. Fox. The guitarist also created an app called Csnaps, which allows people to use their "selfie" obsessions to raise money for their favorite charity.

Main members of the band: Jon Bon Jovi, David Bryan, Tico Torres, Hugh McDonald, Richie Sambora and Alec John Such.

Interesting Band Facts:
- Originally the boys were going to call the band Johnny Electric.
- Desmond Child helped co-write many of the band's greatest hits.
- Tico Torres is a world-renowned professional painter.
- The hit song "You Give Love a Bad Name" was almost given away to fellow rockers Loverboy.
- When *Slippery When Wet* was released, Bon Jovi was actually the opening act for 38 Special.
- Jon has had a very successful solo singing career. His best work coming on the 1990 album *Blaze of Glory*. The title track went to number one on Billboard.
- Jon also delved into acting, where he starred in several well-known movies.
- Richie Sambora released a couple very strong solo albums. The best being *Stranger in This Town*, which featured a guest spot from legend Eric Clapton.
- David Bryan recorded a horror movie soundtrack: *The Netherworld.*
- An initial songwriting session at Richie's childhood home with Jon, Richie, and Desmond immediately produced "You Give Love A Bad Name," which Child secretly reworked from a recent flop he had written for Bonnie Tyler called "If You Were a Woman".

Last Album:
This House Is Not for Sale – 2016
Debuted at number one on Billboard in spite of a flux of new aspects of the band. Phil X played lead guitar after replacing Sambora. Hugh McDonald's role in the band was made

"official" and it was the first BJ album to not be produced by Mercury Records, ending a 32-year relationship.

THINFS received decent critical reviews. The main positive being the band somewhat reverting back to more of a hard/pop rock sound as opposed to the more adult contemporary "soccer mom" country-rock that had become the band's sound over the last decade.

Best Album:
Slippery When Wet – **1986**
After their first two albums Bon Jovi had established themselves as a credible rock band, but nobody was predicting the band's rise to superstar status. Their debut release – *Bon Jovi* – was released in 1984 and produced one semi-hit in "Runaway" (#39 on Billboard). They followed up with *7800 Fahrenheit*, which went Gold and peaked at number 37 on Billboard.

With that modest success and honing their skills with constant touring, Bon Jovi appeared poised to take a step up with their third album. Ratt, Dokken and Motley Crue all released successful albums in 1985. Would Bon Jovi jump up into that realm...or would they remain a solid opening band that had a minor hit with each album?

Jon Bon Jovi has always been known as one of the smarter businessmen in the industry. In 1986 he made a couple really brilliant personnel moves for the band. First, he brought in super-songwriter Desmond Child to help him and Richie write the songs for the album. And then legends Bruce Fairbairn and Bob Rock were brought in to produce and mix it.

How'd that work out for the band? *Slippery When Wet* roared up the Billboard charts to number one, where it stayed for eight weeks (Quiet Riot's *Metal Health* only spent one week at the top). *Slippery* spent more than two years on the Billboard album chart. Three songs cracked the single's top 10. "You Give Love a Bad Name" and "Livin' on a Prayer" both went to number one. "Wanted Dead or Alive" rose all the way to number seven.

Slippery finished as the highest selling album of 1987 and went on to sell close to 30 million copies worldwide. It is still Bon Jovi's top selling album.

Most Underrated Album:
These Days – 1995
Some people attach this label to *Keep the Faith*. But those people are simply wrong. *These Days* is the real masterpiece from Bon Jovi. From top to bottom the heaviest and most mature/intelligent album the band ever released.

Check Out:
"These Days", "It's Hard Letting You Go", "Hearts Breaking Even" and "If That's What It Takes". These songs should have been Bon Jovi classics.

"Bon Jovi is a Solid, hardworking band with great songs that still stand up today," – Mark Knight, Bang Tango

Interesting Facts:
Originally Based: Sayreville, New Jersey
Formed: 1983
Debut Album Released: 1984

Key Albums: *Slippery When Wet* (#3), *New Jersey* (#7), *These Days* (#40), *Bon Jovi* (#63)

Key Songs:
Rock: "Livin' on a Prayer" (#6), "You Give Love a Bad Name" (#21), "Bad Medicine" (#37), "These Days" (#67), "Runaway" (#86), "Keep the Faith" (#89)
Ballad: "Wanted Dead or Alive" (#24), "Never Say Goodbye" (#27), "I'll Be There for You" (#42), "Always" (#46), "Stick To Your Guns" (#59), "Living in Sin" (#79)

Album Rankings:
1. *Slippery When Wet* – 1986
2. *New Jersey* – 1988
3. *These Days* – 1995
4. *Crush* – 2000
5. *Bon Jovi* – 1984
6. *Keep the Faith* – 1992
7. *7800 Fahrenheit* – 1985
8. *Bounce* – 2002
9. *Have a Nice Day* – 2005
10. *Burning Bridges* – 2015

Top Songs:
1. "Living on a Prayer" – *Slippery When Wet*
2. "Wanted Dead or Alive" – *Slippery When Wet*
3. "You Give Love a Bad Name" – *Slippery When Wet*
4. "Bad Medicine" – *New Jersey*
5. "These Days" – *These Days*
6. "Runaway" – *Bon Jovi*
7. "Keep the Faith" – *Keep the Faith*
8. "Never Say Goodbye" – *Slippery When Wet*
9. "Wild in the Streets" – *Slippery When Wet*
10. "Lay Your Hands on Me" – *New Jersey*

11. "It's My Life" – *Crush*
12. "I'll Be There for You" – *New Jersey*
13. "I'm With You" – *What About Now*
14. "Hearts Breaking Even" – *These Days*
15. "In and Out of Love" – *7800 Fahrenheit*
16. "Always" – *Cross Road*
17. "If That's What It Takes" – *These Days*
18. "Everyday" – *Bounce*
19. "Stick to Your Guns" – *New Jersey*
20. "She Don't Know Me" – *Bon Jovi*
21. "We Don't Run" – *Burning Bridges*
22. "Edge of a Broken Heart" – *Disorderlies Soundtrack*
23. "Born to Be My Baby" – *New Jersey*
24. "Living in Sin" – *New Jersey*
25. "Misunderstood" – *Bounce*
26. "What Do You Got" – *Greatest Hits*
27. "Who Says You Can't Go Home" – *Have a Nice Day*
28. "Someday I'll Be Saturday Night" – *Cross Road*
29. "Wild Is the Wind" – *New Jersey*
30. "Have a Nice Day" – *Have a Nice Day*

Guns N' Roses

GnR is easily one of the greatest rock bands of all time, regardless of what genre you are talking about. They were the best rock band in the world in 1987–88…in 1991–1993, and again, amazingly enough, in 2017–2018! GnR's *Use Your Illusion* tour broke rock touring records in the early 90s. Their current world tour has been labeled as the second most successful grossing tour in music history. There is a legitimate case to be made that Guns N' Roses are the overall best rock band of all time.

The only thing that keeps Guns from blowing away their competition – Stones, Beatles, Zeppelin and a couple others – is a relatively small output of albums. Axl Rose is the most dynamic and exciting singer of the entire genre. Throw in Slash's guitar riffs, Izzy's writing skills, Duff's punk vibe and Adler's swing behind the kit and the result is the greatest album of the entire HM/HB genre. *Appetite for Destruction* might be the best rock album ever released.

GnR really dominated the Billboard 200. They had two albums go to #1, two albums go to #2 and two albums go to #3! GnR is so good that their *Greatest Hits* album sold more than five million copies and spent years on the Billboard album charts. GnR placed eleven songs in the top 200 of our rock list and had four ballads on the top 100 of our slow songs list!

Guns' first album *Appetite for Destruction* is the best-selling debut album of all time, and also one of the top 20 best-selling albums in history. The band then shocked the music world with their next official non–EP release. GnR put out *Use Your Illusion I* and *II* on the same day. Tens of thousands of fans lined up for hours to be able to purchase the two albums when record stores had a special midnight opening. The Illusions debuted at number one and two on Billboard, the only time in music history the same band held the top two spots.

GnR is the second best-selling band of the genre. Their YouTube videos for "November Rain" and "Sweet Child O' Mine" both recently passed one billion views. "November Rain" was the first music video released in the 1990s to reach that mark.

Interesting Band Facts:
- Axl once contemplated naming the band AIDS.
- Tracii Guns and Axl Rose formed the early version of Guns N' Roses. Rose's GnR has had more than 20 different lineups, while Tracii's L.A. Guns has had more than 30.
- On the band's first tour: The Hell Tour – the band's 1988 Oldsmobile broke down and they were forced to abandon most of their gear and hitchhike to Seattle.
- During the early years, the band was riding in Duff's Celica and were t–boned by a car going 60 mph. Amazingly, only Adler was injured (broken ankle).
- Slash's mother once dated David Bowie, who later visited GnR and flirted with Axl's girlfriend and future wife Erin Everly. Axl took a swing at the Hall of Fame legend over the flirting. The two icons quickly made up though.
- Axl Rose is an anagram of "oral sex".
- In his younger days Slash was a professional talent level BMX biker.

- *Appetite for Destruction* is still the top selling debut album of all time, moving more than 30 million units.
- Axl reportedly worked on the epic "November Rain" for ten years before its 1991 release.
- As a young boy Axl sang in the church choir.
- GnR's first single was "It's So Easy"…released in the UK. A couple months later the band released "Welcome to the Jungle" in the US. It took almost a full year before "Jungle" became a smash hit.
- GnR has had only one number Billboard song: "Sweet Child O' Mine" which was one of the quickest written songs by the band.
- Axl and Izzy both grew up in the same town: Lafayette, Indiana.
- The two were so broke at one point they participated in a smoking medical study at UCLA for $8 an hour.
- Axl reportedly has the greatest vocal range of any singer in rock history. His five-octave range is better than Mariah Carey's.
- Axl once traveled with a professional psychic who the rest of the band nicknamed Yoda. She would test rooms to see if they had bad or good vibes before Axl would enter them.
- The moaning sounds in "Rocket Queen" are real. Apparently Axl had sex with Adler's girlfriend and recorded the pleasure moans.

Last Album / Most Underrated Album:
Chinese Democracy – 2008

What a long, strange, crazy journey *Chinese Democracy* turned out to be. Once labeled the most anticipated album of all time, *CD* was met with a wide range of opinions. Some fans hailed it as Axl's genius at work...others wouldn't even listen to it since there was no Slash, Duff or Izzy involvement.

CD did fairly well on the business side, reaching number three on Billboard and selling several million copies. Critics (like fans) either loved or hated it. The biggest complaints about Axl's GnR album were the aforementioned lack of involvement from past members (most notably Slash) and that Axl took an amazing raw 1999 album and tinkered with it to death, adding layer after layer after layer of sound.

On the positive note, if people can get by their pro–Slash/Izzy bias, standing on its own merits *Chinese Democracy* is a pretty great rock album. "Better", "TWAT", "Street of Dreams", "Madagascar" and "Catcher in the Rye" sound like they could have been on the follow up album to the *Illusions*. "Riad N' the Bedouins" is a kick–ass rocker. "Chinese Democracy" and "Sorry" are grown up Axl Rose songs. "Prostitute" is a solid ballad. And songs like "Shackler's Revenge", "This I Love" and "Scraped" were fun songs in the sense that Axl didn't just recreate an 80's rock album, but experimented a bit and had a little fun.

Best Album:
Appetite for Destruction – 1987

The greatest selling debut album of all time might be the best rock album ever released. Axl's unique and powerful voice, Slash's iconic guitar riffs and Izzy's underrated song writing produced an album that still holds up today. We ranked *Appetite* as the best Hair Metal album of all time.

"Great first record. The original band had amazing chemistry and captured the raw essence of a real rock and roll band," – Mark Knight, Bang Tango.

Appetite spent five weeks at number one on the Billboard album chart, where it stayed ranked for an incredible 204 weeks. Even more amazing, 29 years after dominating the Billboard 200, *Appetite* snuck back into the top 10.

Three songs off of *Appetite* made the single's top 10 – including "Sweet Child O' Mine" going to number one.

"I absolutely love GnR, *Appetite* changed my life," – Nick Walsh, Slik Toxik.

Everything about the album is iconic. "Welcome to the Jungle" is the most played rock song in history, having parts of it featured in pretty much every sporting event – from high school to professional – in the world. Who can ever forget Axl's screeching demon–filled vocals? Or Slash's top hat and ripping guitar work? "SCOM" is the ultimate power ballad. "Paradise City" is the perfect summer party song for true rockers.

Objectively, 10 of the 12 songs on *Appetite* are fantastic rock songs. And we haven't even mentioned the song a lot of people feel is GnR's most underrated tune: "Rocket Queen"!

"I loved *Appetite* and how it set them apart from all the safe, clean, boring 80's hair rock that was being regurgitated. All of the sudden every band got a little dirtier and loved bandanas!" – Brian Tichy, Whitesnake & Ozzy.

Appetite topped our list as the best album of the genre. While "Welcome to the Jungle" earned the number one spot on our Best Songs of the genre list.

"(Welcome to the Jungle) great song – started the whole ball rolling," – Jeff Pilson, Dokken. "Magical band when the chemistry is right."

Interesting Facts:
Originally Based: Los Angeles, CA
Formed: 1985
Debut Album Released: 1987

Main members of the band include:
Axl Rose, Slash, Duff McKagan, Dizzy Reed, Matt Sorum and Izzy Stradlin.

Other key members that have played with the band include:
Richard Fortus, Frank Ferrer, Gilby Clarke, Robin Finck, Tommy Stinson, Buckethead, Ron Thal and DJ Ashba.

Key Albums:
Appetite for Destruction (#1), *Use Your Illusion II* (#8), *Use Your Illusion I* (#30), *Chinese Democracy* (#75), *Lies* (#94)

Key Songs:
Rock: "Welcome to the Jungle" (#1), "Sweet Child O' Mine" (#14), "You Could Be Mine" (#36), "Paradise City" (#59), "Civil War" (#96)

Ballad: "November Rain" (#2), "Don't Cry" (#16), "Patience" (#28), "Estranged" (#47)

Top Songs:
1. "Welcome to the Jungle" – *Appetite for Destruction*
2. "Sweet Child O' Mine" – *Appetite for Destruction*
3. "You Could Be Mine" – *Use Your Illusion II*
4. "November Rain" – *Use Your Illusion I*
5. "Paradise City" – *Appetite for Destruction*
6. "Better" – *Chinese Democracy*
7. "Civil War" – *Use Your Illusion II*
8. "Nightrain" – *Appetite for Destruction*
9. "Estranged" – *Use Your Illusion II*
10. "Rocket Queen" – *Appetite for Destruction*
11. "Don't Cry" – *Use Your Illusion I*
12. "Patience" – *Lies*
13. "Knockin' On Heaven's Door" – *Days of Thunder* soundtrack
14. "Yesterdays" – *Use Your Illusion II*
15. "TWAT" – *Chinese Democracy*
16. "Pretty Tied Up" – *Use Your Illusion II*
17. "Live and Let Die" – *Use Your Illusion I*
18. "It's So Easy" – *Appetite for Destruction*
19. "My Michelle" – *Appetite for Destruction*
20. "Reckless Life" – *Lies*
21. "Street of Dreams" – *Chinese Democracy*
22. "Used to Love Her" – *Lies*
23. "Coma" – *Use Your Illusion I*
24. "Don't Damn Me" – *Use Your Illusion I*
25. "Oh My God" – *End of Days* soundtrack

Def Leppard

Joe Elliott and company debuted in all the way back in 1977! But they are still headlining tours and putting out successful albums today! Def Leppard is one of the more fascinating bands of the genre. They started off as a metal band, standing beside greats like AC/DC and Judas Priest. Then they softened their sound a little and released the masterpiece *Pyromania*. The band then transformed from a hair metal band to more of a pop hair band when they released a second classic album – *Hysteria*.

Leppard has the second most songs on our Top 1,000 list, trailing only Bon Jovi. And they finished with the second and fourth best albums of the entire genre. Def Leppard also owned the Billboard charts during their long career, scoring two #1 albums and albums topping out at #2 and #5. All in all DL has had seven albums crack the top 10 albums chart.

Def Leppard is the third highest selling band of the genre. And it can be argued that Def Leppard might have been the catalyst for both styles of the genre: hair metal and hair band music. *Pyromania* was an amazing rock album. Released in 1983, *Pyromania* added a slight pop edge to an AC/DC / Van Halen rock sound – basically creating the hair metal music genre. But then the band took a 180 and went the pure slick pop–rock route with the 1987 release of *Hysteria*, which might be the best 'hair band' album of all time.

Best Album:
***Pyromania* – 1983**
Younger Def Leppard fans will be screaming "WTF!" when they see *Pyromania* listed instead of *Hysteria*. And we feel

you. But in our humble and objective opinion *Pyromania* is the near perfect album. *Hysteria* is one of the most popular hair band and rock albums of all time. But *Pyromania* was life-changing.

For perspective, the top single of 1982 was "Physical" by Olivia Newton-John. Other songs to make the top 10 were "Ebony and Ivory" by Paul McCartney and Stevie Wonder, "Don't You Want Me" by The Human League and "Hard to Say I'm Sorry" by Chicago. Then along comes Def Leppard with *Pyromania*. Millions of young teenagers were craving some classic hard rock music and *Pyromania* filled that need 100-fold.

"Photograph" was the song to knock Michael Jackson off the top of the charts. "Rock of Ages", "Foolin'" and "Too Late For Love" are all hard-rock masterpieces.

Pyromania spent 123 weeks on the Billboard 200.

Last Album:
Def Leppard **– 2015**
In 2015 Def Leppard released their self-titled album, which surprised music critics by busting into the top 10 on the Billboard album charts. After years of releasing albums of various creative styles, the band went back to their late 80s roots and released a pretty strong rock album. We had it ranked as the seventh best album of the year.

"Blind Faith" topped our 2015 Best Ballads of the Year chart. "Sea of Love" was the highest-ranking rocker.

Most Underrated Album:
High 'n' Dry – 1981

The band's last album with the incredible Pete Willis tops our list as Def Leppard's most underrated album. Released in 1981, *High 'n' Dry* appeared to set Def Leppard up as the world's next superstar hard rock / metal superstars. (Before *Pyromania* and *Hysteria* softened the band's overall sound).

"Let It Go" influenced about 50% of all the harder songs of the hair metal genre. Cinderella owes their career to "Let It Go". Other great songs include "Bringin' On the Heartbreak", "Lady Strange", "You Got Me Runnin'" and "On Through the Night".

Interesting Band Notes:
- Phil Collen was just 14 when he attended his first concert – Deep Purple in London in 1972. Years later, examining the back cover of Deep Purple's *Made in Japan* album, Collen saw himself in the front row!
- In 1984 Rick Allen was involved in a horrible car crash that cost the drummer his arm. One good outcome came from the crash. Allen ended up marrying the lady (a nurse) who arrived at the crash scene and helped save Allen's life.
- Allen's mom replied to an ad titled "Leppard Loses Skins" on behalf of her 14-year-old son. Allen was offered the job on his 15th birthday. He dropped out of school and the rest is history.
- Def Leppard is one of only five rock bands that have had two studio albums sell more than 10 million copies in the U.S.

- The Def Leppard boys took a loan from Joe Elliott's father and started their own label to promote their debut album. The album sold like hot cakes, sparking a bidding war by several major labels.
- Hysteria had seven singles chart on Billboard. The album remained on the Album charts for almost three years.
- Joe Elliott fronts a Mott The Hoople cover band.
- Thomas Dolby plays keyboards on the album *Pyromania*. He is credited as Booker T. Boffin.
- Mutt Lange was a co-writer on every song on *Pyromania* and *Hysteria*.
- Joe Elliott auditioned for Atomic Mass as a guitar player. During the audition the rest of the band decided Elliott was too good of a singer and hired him to handle vocals. That band morphed into Def Leppard.
- Def Leppard earned a spot in the Guinness Book of World Records after playing shows on three different continents in one day (Morocco, England and Canada).

Def Leppard Facts:
Originally based out of Sheffield, South Yorkshire. Formed in 1977, debut album released in 1980.

Main members of the band include:
Joe Elliott, Rick Savage, Rick Allen, Pete Willis, Steve Clark, Phil Collen and Vivian Campbell.

Key Albums:
Pyromania (#2), *Hysteria* (#5), *High 'n' Dry* (#31), *Adrenalize* (#56)

Key Songs:
Rock: "Photograph" (#2), "Pour Some Sugar On Me" (#7), "Rock of Ages" (#18), "Let it Go" (#20), "Foolin'" (#42), "Too Late for Love" (#73), "Lady Strange" (#100)
Ballad: "Hysteria" (#6), "Bringin' On the Heartbreak" (#8), "Love Bites" (#81)

Top Songs:
1. "Photograph" – *Pyromania*
2. "Pour Some Sugar On Me" – *Hysteria*
3. "Rock of Ages" – *Pyromania*
4. "Bringin' On the Heartbreak" – *High 'n' Dry*
5. "Let It Go" – *High 'n' Dry*
6. "Foolin'" – *Pyromania*
7. "Lady Strange" – *High 'n' Dry*
8. "Too Late for Love" – *Pyromania*
9. "Hysteria" – *Hysteria*
10. "Rock Rock" – *Pyromania*
11. "Love Bites" – *Hysteria*
12. "Armageddon It" – *Hysteria*
13. "Women" – *Hysteria*
14. "Tonight" – *Adrenalize*
15. "Rocket" – *Hysteria*
16. "All I Want Is Everything" – *Slang*
17. "Fractured Love" – *Retro Active*
18. "Undefeated" – *Mirror Ball – Live & More*
19. "Torn To Shreds" – *X*
20. "Long, Long Way to Go" – *X*
21. "Work It Out" – *Slang*
22. "Sea of Love" – *Def Leppard*
23. "Let's Get Rocked" – *Adrenalize*
24. "Tomorrow" – *Songs from The Sparkle Lounge*
25. "Have You Ever Needed Someone So Bad" – *Adrenalize*

Motley Crue

Like Def Leppard, Motley was one of the bands that helped spark both the hair metal and hair band craze! They transformed their look for each album and are one of the bands that really embraced the rock 'n' roll lifestyle. Vince Neil didn't have the best voice, Mick Mars wasn't a Guitar God and nobody has ever claimed that Nikki Sixx and Tommy Lee were revolutionary artists with their instruments. But Motley had the sound, the look, the attitude and most importantly they started music trends as opposed to the bands that followed whatever was popular.

The really great thing about Motley during their prime was the diversity in each album release. Every album sounded like classic Crue but had a different style than the prior one. They were one of the few bands that didn't just rewrite each album over and over again.

Motley Crue changed their sound on every album. Their sleazy sound is our favorite.

Nikki Sixx was the workhorse of the band. He was the band's main songwriter, promoter, manager, publicist…basically anything that needed to be done to make a band successful, Sixx was the motivating force.

Drummer Tommy Lee has lived the true Rockstar life. Vince Neil is an amazing studio vocalist. And older statesmen Mick Mars' guitar hooks and solos really gave the Motley Crue sound substance.

"Mick Mars is a legend in his own right. He has his own vibe that isn't a copy of the usual suspects. He's more old school like Hendrix. He was awesome," Jay Pepper, Tigertailz.

Motley sold the fourth most albums of any band on our list.

Motley released 10 albums that made the Billboard top 20 and had seven songs break into the top 40 on the singles chart. Motley had the most songs chart in the top 200 of our Top 1,000 list!

"Motley Crue: Cool fucking Hollywood rock–n–roll," – Brian Young, Beau Nasty.

Best Album:
***Shout at the Devil* – 1983**
Dr. Feelgood was the most successful album of Motley Crue's career and had some of the band's most mature and sophisticated work. But it also features several songs that are pure fillers. One good definition of a filler is a song that will never be played live, and as fantastic as *Feelgood* is the album has several of them.

Shout at the Devil, on the other hand, is 35 minutes of pure perfection Well, 32 minutes. The only stain is the album's final song "Danger".

Rock kids were flooded with safe pop music in 1983 before *Shout* was released. Michael Jackson, The Police, Irene Cara, Bonnie Tyler, Hall & Oates and Men at Work ruled the charts. Then stepped up Motley Crue, with each member dressed in chains and leather, scary face makeup and songs about the devil and kicking ass. Teenage kids ate up the sleazy Los Angeles themed metal.

Last Album
***Saints of Los Angeles* 2008 / *The Dirt* 2019**
Saints of Los Angeles is Motley's last full-length album release. The band dropped it in 2008 and *SOLA* promptly went to number four on Billboard and the title song reached number five on the Rock charts. The album was supposed to represent Motley's career in Los Angeles, with each song having a specific meaning to the band's earlier career.

Motley became extremely relevant again in 2019 with the movie release of their biography – *The Dirt* – and the soundtrack to the popular movie.

The Dirt debuted at #10 on Billboard and featured three brand new songs, as well as an unusual cover of Madonna's "Like a Virgin".

Most Underrated Album:
***Too Fast for Love* – 1981**
In our opinion this is Motley Crue's true masterpiece. It's pure sleaze, raw emotion and there was no other band in the world that sounded like them. Rolling Stone recently ranked Too Fast For Love as the 22nd best metal album of all time.

Songs that should be on your iPod include "On With The Show", "Too Fast for Love", "Live Wire", "Starry Eyes" and "Merry–Go–Round". The entire album is pure magic.

Interesting Band Notes:
- Vince Neil initially blew off his audition for Motley. Luckily, he later changed his mind and joined the band.

- Nikki Sixx wrote "Without You" after watching the love affair between Tommy Lee and Heather Locklear.
- "Home Sweet Home" was released twice by the band. Surprisingly enough, the 1991 re-release out charted the original 1985 version.
- The song "Kickstart My Heart" is an actual written account of bassist and songwriter Nikki Sixx's brush with death.
- Vince starred in a reality show on the WB in 2003 called *The Surreal Life*. He was joined by "stars" like MC Hammer, Corey Feldman, and Emanuel Lewis
- Stephen Pearcy (of Ratt fame) was offered the job as lead singer by Nikki Sixx in 1981.
- Motley Crue only opened for Kiss for five shows before they were kicked off the tour by Gene Simmons. Reportedly, Simmons was unhappy with the band`s behavior. But many think it was because but Crue was outshining Kiss onstage.
- Vince quit Motley Crue in 1992 and spent years driving race cars. He competed in the Indy Lights races at Long Beach, Milwaukee, Phoenix and Portland. His best finish was 10th at Milwaukee.

Motley Crue Facts:
Originally Based: Los Angeles, CA
Formed: 1981
Debut Album Released: 1981

Main members of the band include:
Mick Mars, Nikki Sixx, Vince Neil, Tommy Lee, and John Corabi

Other members included:
Randy Castillo and Samantha Maloney.

Key Albums:
Girls, Girls, Girls (#6), *Dr. Feelgood* (#9), *Too Fast for Love* (#15), *Shout at the Devil* (19), *Theatre of Pain* (#61), *Motley Crue* (#67),

Key Songs:
Rock: "Shout at the Devil" (#10), "Dr. Feelgood" (#13), "Looks That Kill" (#24), "Girls, Girls, Girls" (#28), "Wildside" (#33), "Don't Go Away Mad" (#35), "Live Wire" (#39), "Kickstart My Heart" (#43), "Too Fast for Love" (#51)
Ballad: "Home Sweet Home" (#11), "You're All I Need" (#32), "On With the Show" (#35)

Top Songs
1. "Shout at the Devil" – *Shout at the Devil*
2. "Dr. Feelgood" – *Dr. Feelgood*
3. "Looks That Kill" – *Shout at the Devil*
4. "Live Wire" – *Too Fast for Love*
5. "Girls, Girls, Girls" – *Girls, Girls, Girls*
6. "Home Sweet Home" – *Theatre of Pain*
7. "Wild Side" – *Girls, Girls, Girls*,
8. "Don't Go Away Mad" – *Dr. Feelgood*
9. "Too Fast for Love" – *Too Fast for Love*
10. "Kickstart My Heart" – *Dr. Feelgood*
11. "Too Young to Fall In Love" – *Shout at the Devil*
12. "On with the Show" – *Too Fast For Love*
13. "Smoking in the Boy's Room" – *Theatre of Pain*
14. "S.O.S." – *Dr. Feelgood*
15. "Primal Scream" – *Decade of Decadence*
16. "Bitter Pill" – *Greatest Hits*
17. "Hooligan's Holiday" – *Motley Crue*

18. "If I Die Tomorrow" – *Red, White & Crue*
19. "Misunderstood" – *Motley Crue*
20. "Hollywood Ending" – *New Tattoo*
21. "Tonight" – *Too Fast for Love*
22. "City Boy Blues" – *Theatre of Pain*
23. "Driftaway" – *Motley Crue*
24. "You're All I Need" – *Girls, Girls, Girls*
25. "New Tattoo" – *New Tattoo*

Album Rankings:
1. *Girls, Girls, Girls* – 1987
2. *Dr. Feelgood* – 1989
3. *Too Fast for Love* – 1981
4. *Shout at the Devil* – 1983
5. *Motley Crue* – 1994
6. *Theatre of Pain* – 1985
7. *New Tattoo* – 2000
8. *Saints of Los Angeles* – 2008
9. *Generation Swine* – 1997

THEATRE HEADLINERS

The following bands are legends of the genre. They could headline theatre tours and clubs or be great opening acts for the Big Four bands listed above. To make this group a band had to have more than just one song or one album do well on Billboard. They had to have at least a couple iconic songs or iconic band members, plus have multiple songs/albums in our Top 1,000 songs / Top 350 albums chart.

These bands share the second floor of the Hall of Fame building.

Tesla

Tesla is one of those bands that is more of an old fashion hard rock group. But they get attached to the HM/HB era simply because their career path exploded during the 80s and 90s.

Jeff Keith's vocals helped Tesla produce five albums that charted in the top 25 on Billboard, which included two songs that made the Hot 100 top 10 list. They also finished with 31 songs on our Top 1,000 list – the fifth highest total of any band.

Tesla's first four albums were stronger than 99% of their contemporaries. Keith's rock vocals combined with the killer (and extremely underrated) dual guitar attack of Frank Hannon and Tommy Skeoch gave the band a hardness that almost no other hair metal band possessed. Tesla were one of the few bands that concentrated on putting out awesome full length albums that needed to be listened to from start to finish, as opposed to so many bands that released albums that had 3–4 strong singles and then the rest of the album was mostly filler. *Mechanical Resonance*, *Psychotic Supper*, *Bust a Nut* and *The Great Radio Controversy* were all ranked on our top 40 albums of all-time list.

We selected "Love Song" was as the greatest ballad of all time. Tesla finished with six songs ranked in our top 100 rock songs list.

Tesla Facts:
Interesting Facts:
Originally Based: Sacramento, CA
Formed: 1981
Debut Album Released: 1986

Main band members include:
Brian Wheat, Frank Hannon, Jeff Keith, Troy Luccketta, Dave Rude and Tommy Skeoch.

Albums: Best, Most Underrated, Last:
Best: *Mechanical Resonance – 1986*
Most Underrated: *Psychotic Supper* – 1991
Last: *Shock* – 2019

Key Albums:
Mechanical Resonance (#23), *Psychotic Supper* (#29), *Bust a Nut* (#39)

Key Songs:
Rock: "Little Suzi" (#49), "Signs" (#61), "Caught in a Dream" (#80), "Stir It Up" (#89)
Ballad: "Love Song" (#1), "Try So Hard" (#43)

Top Songs
1. "Love Song" – *Great Radio Controversy*
2. "Little Susie" – *Mechanical Resonance*
3. "Stir It Up" – *Psychotic Supper*
4. "Signs" – *Five Man Acoustical Jam*
5. "Caught in a Dream" – *Into the Now*
6. "Need Your Lovin'" – *Bust a Nut*
7. "Modern Day Cowboys" – *Mechanical Resonance*
8. "Edison's Medicine" – *Psychotic Supper*
9. "Getting Better" – *Mechanical Resonance*
10. "The Way It Is" – *The Great Radio Controversy*
11. "Try So Hard" – *Bust a Nut*
12. "Forever More" – *Forever More*
13. "So Divine" – *Simplicity*
14. "2nd Street" – *Twisted Wires & The Acoustic Sessions*
15. "Hang Tough" – *The Great Radio Controversy*
16. "Call It What You Want" – *Psychotic Summer*
17. "Words Can't Explain" – *Into the Now*
18. "Mama's Fool" – *Bust a Nut*
19. "So What" – *Forever More*
20. "Fallin' Apart" – *Forever More*

Album Rankings:
1. *Mechanical Resonance* – 1986
2. *Psychotic Supper* – 1991
3. *Bust a Nut* – 1994
4. *The Great Radio Controversy* – 1989
5. *Into the Now* – 2004
6. *Five Man Acoustical Jam* – 1990
7. *Forever More* – 2008
8. *Twisted Wires & The Acoustic Sessions* – 2011
9. *Simplicity* – 2014
10. *Reel to Reel I & II* – 2007

Whitesnake

David Coverdale. "Still of the Night". Tawny Kitaen. Enough said.

Whitesnake are one of the older statesmen of the genre. They started building their skills and resume in the 70s. By the time the HM/HB ruled the rock world, Whitesnake was a fine–tuned, well–oiled rock 'n' roll powerhouse who kicked as much ass as anybody.

"David is a legendary singer who when I first heard on MTV singing "Slow and Easy" I was like "wtf"! What a badass voice! He's also a great guy," – Brian Tichy, who spent three years drumming for Whitesnake.

Coverdale also was the lead singer for the band Deep Purple.

Whitesnake scored a number one and number two song on the Billboard Hot 100 charts, as well as scoring two top 10 albums! Whitesnake also dominates our local charts, the self–titled 1987 album tied a record (with several other bands) having seven songs that made our Top 1,000 list!

We ranked "Still of the Night" as the ninth best rock song in history.

Main band members include:
David Coverdale, Tommy Aldridge, Reb Beach, Adrian Vandenberg, Neil Murray, Rudy Sarzo, Micky Moody, Vivian Campbell and Jon Lord.

Whitesnake Facts:
Originally Based: Middlesbrough, Cleveland, England
Formed: 1978
Debut Album Released: 1978

Albums: Best, Most Underrated, Last:
Best: *Whitesnake* – 1987
Most Underrated: *Saints & Sinners* – 1982
Last: *Flesh & Blood* – 2019

Key Albums:
Whitesnake (#13), *Slide It In* (#60)

Key Songs:
Rock: "Still of the Night" (#9), "Fool For Your Loving" (#40), "Slow and Easy" (#102)
Ballad: "Here I Go Again" (#9), "Is This Love" (#69), "Too Many Tears" (#72)

Top Songs:
1. "Still of the Night" – *Whitesnake*
2. "Fool for Your Loving" – *Ready an' Willing*
3. "Slow and Easy" – *Slide It In*
4. "Here I Go Again" – *Whitesnake*
5. "Slide It In" – *Slide It In*
6. "Lay Down Your Love" – *Good to Be Bad*
7. "Give Me All Your Love" – *Whitesnake*
8. "Is This Love" – *Whitesnake*
9. "Can You Hear the Wind Blow" – *Good to Be Bad*
10. "Bad Boys" – *Whitesnake*
11. "Too Many Tears" – *Restless Heart*
12. "All for Love" – *Good to Be Bad*
13. "Steal Your Heart Away" – *Forevermore*
14. "Summer Rain" – *Good to Be Bad*

15. "Crying" – *Restless Heart*
16. "All Out of Luck" – *Forevermore*
17. "The Deeper the Love" – *Slip of the Tongue*
18. "I Need You" – *Forevermore*
19. "All I Want All I Need" – *Good to Be Bad*
20. "Fool in Love Again" – *Good to Be Bad*

Album Rankings:
1. *Whitesnake* – 1987
2. *Saints & Sinners* – 1982
3. *Ready an' Willing* – 1980
4. *Slide It In* – 1984
5. *Slip of the Tongue* – 1989
6. *Restless Heart* – 1997
7. *Forevermore* – 2011
8. *Good to Be Bad* – 2008

Skid Row

The heaviest band on the list! Skid Row was well on their way to becoming one of the upper echelon bands of not just the HM/HB genre, but all of rock music. They were hard, heavy and also had a pop–sensibility and could write killer ballads.

Unfortunately, the band split with lead singer Sebastian Bach and even though they continued to release solid albums, Skid Row were never able to capture the same magic as their first couple of releases. Very few bands can match the overall output of Skid Row's first two album punch of *Skid Row* and *Slave to the Grind*.

Skid Row had two top 10 albums on Billboard, as well as two songs that also cracked the top 10. *Slave to the Grind* reached the number one spot on the album chart.

They also dominated our Top 1,000 list, battling the big boys for the number one spot on all three charts (album, rock, ballads). Def Leppard, Motley Crue, Guns N' Roses and Skid Row were the only four bands to rank in the top 10 in all three of those categories.

Guitar player Dave Sabo was childhood friends with Jon Bon Jovi. The two promised each other that if either made it big in the music world they would take care of the other one. Sabo was a member of the band Bon Jovi when they toured the song Runaway, before he was later replaced by Richie Sambora.

Sabo and bass player Rachel Bolan are the band's main songwriters.

Skid Row Facts:
Originally Based: Toms River, NJ
Formed: 1986
Debut Album Released: 1989

Main band members include:
Dave Sabo, Rachel Bolan, Scotti Hill, Sebastian Bach, Rob Hammersmith, Rob Affuso, Johnny Solinger.

Albums: Best, Most Underrated, Last:
Best: *Skid Row* – 1989
Most Underrated: *Subhuman Race* – 1995
Last: *Rise of the Damnation Army* – 2014

Key Albums:
Skid Row (#5), *Slave to the Grind* (#10)

Key Songs:
Rock: "18 and Life" (#8), "Youth Gone Wild" (#15), "Monkey Business" (#44), "Piece of Me" (#74), "Slave to the Grind" (#83)
Ballad: "I Remember You" (#3), "Breakin' Down" (#36), "Wasted Time" (#44)

Top Songs:
1. "18 and Life" – *Skid Row*
2. "Youth Gone Wild" – *Skid Row*
3. "Slave to the Grind" – *Slave to the Grind*
4. "I Remember You" – *Skid Row*
5. "Piece of Me" – *Skid Row*
6. "Monkey Business" – *Slave to the Grind*
7. "Big Guns" – *Skid Row*
8. "Breakin' Down" – *Subhuman Race*

9. "Wasted Time" – *Slave to the Grind*
10. "Riot Act" – *Slave to the Grind*
11. "In a Darkened Room" – *Slave to the Grind*
12. "Stitches" – *United World Rebellion Chapter One*
13. "See You Around" – *Thickskin*
14. "This Is Killing Me" – *United World Rebellion Chapter One*
15. "Give It the Gun" – *United World Rebellion Chapter Two*
16. "Kings of Demolition" – *United World Rebellion Chapter One*
17. "Forever" – *40 Seasons*
18. "Catch Your Fall" – *United World Rebellion Chapter Two*

Album Rankings:
1. *Skid Row* – 1989
2. *Slave to the Grind* – 1991
3. *Subhuman Race* – 1995
4. *United World Rebellion Chapter One* – 2013
5. *Rise of the Damnation Army – United World Rebellion Chapter Two* – 2014
6. *Thickskin* – 2003

L.A. Guns

Just a good, old–fashion rock and roll sleaze band! Tracii Guns was briefly in Guns N' Roses before splitting with Axl Rose and forming L.A. Guns. While the band didn't reach the success of GnR, L.A. Guns has been one of the most solid bands of the entire HM/HB era. Almost every album the band releases is full of great songs – whether it's 1988 or 2017.

L.A. Guns charted three albums in the top 50 on the Billboard 200 chart. They were one of the eight bands to end up with 30 or more songs on our top 1,000 list.

In terms of our personal rankings, L.A. Guns has been the most successful legendary 80s band in the 2000s. We ranked *The Missing Peace* as the best rock album of 2017 and "The Devil Made Me Do It" as the year's best song. For 2012, we ranked *Hollywood Forever* as the year's best album. And in 2002, we put *Waking the Dead* as the year's best album and "Don't You Cry" as the best song.

L.A. Guns Facts:
Originally Based: Los Angeles, CA
Formed: 1983
Debut Album Released: 1988

Main band members include: Tracii Guns, Phil Lewis, Adam Hamilton, Mick Cripps, Kelly Nickels, Steve Riley, Stacey Blades. L.A. Guns has had more than 40 members, so apologies if we missed a major player. There have been three different versions of the band, which have amazingly have featured a total of 49 different lineups. Fourteen different singers have fronted a version of the band.

Albums: Best, Most Underrated, Last:
Best: *L.A. Guns* – 1988
Most Underrated: *The Missing Peace* – 2017
Last: *The Devil You Know* – 2019

Key Albums:
L.A. Guns (#22), *Cocked & Loaded* (#36), *Waking the Dead* (#42), *Hollywood Vampires* (#87)

Key Songs:
Rock: "Electric Gypsy" (#17), "One More Reason" (#38), "Never Enough" (#63)
Ballad: "Ballad of Jayne" (#21), "Dreamtime" (#61)

Top Songs:
1. "Electric Gypsy" – *L.A. Guns*
2. "One More Reason" – *L.A. Guns*
3. "Never Enough" – *Cocked & Loaded*
4. "Ballad of Jayne" – *Cocked & Loaded*
5. "It's Over Now" – *Hollywood Vampires*
6. "Sex Action" – *L.A. Guns*
7. "Kiss My Love Goodbye" – *Hollywood Vampires*
8. "I Wanna Be Your Man" – *Cocked & Loaded*
9. "Don't You Cry" – *Waking the Dead*
10. "The Devil Made Me Do It" – *The Missing Piece*
11. "Dreamtime" – *Shrinking Violet*
12. "City of Angels" – *Waking the Dead*
13. "Beautiful" – *Man in the Moon*
14. "Why Ain't I Bleeding" – *Vicious Circle*
15. "Wasted" – *Wasted*
16. "Revolution" – *Waking the Dead*
17. "Nothing Better to Do" – *Vicious Circle*
18. "Hollywood Forever" – *Hollywood Forever*

19. "No Crime" – *Vicious Circle*
20. "Kiss of Death" – *Vicious Circle*

Top Albums:
1. *L.A. Guns* – 1988
2. *Cocked & Loaded* – 1989
3. *Waking the Dead* – 2002
4. *Hollywood Forever* – 2012
5. *The Missing Peace* – 2017
6. *Hollywood Vampires* – 1991
7. *Vicious Circle* – 1994
8. *Man in the Moon* – 2001
9. *Tales From the Strip* – 2005
10. *Shrinking Violet* – 1999

Warrant

Jani Lane is often cited as one of the best – if not the best – songwriters of the entire HM/HB genre. Warrant produced a couple of the most iconic songs and videos of the era. Their *Dog Eat Dog* album is an underrated masterpiece! And who can ever forget the video for "Cherry Pie"?

Warrant charted three top 25 albums on Billboard and had three songs break into the single's top 10. They finished with more than 30 songs in our Top 1,000 song list, one of only eight bands to break the 30-song mark!

"We have played a lot of shows with Warrant. They are good guys and a great band," – Paul Taylor, Winger.

Warrant's first four albums were all really great and also showed a real growth within the band. *Dirty Rotten Filthy Stinking Rich* was pure hair metal cheese, but produced four songs that charted on Billboard. The follow-up *Cherry Pie* went all the way to #7 on the Billboard 200 and featured a more mature version of the band with songs like "Uncle Tom's Cabin" and "I Saw Red". Their third album was a hair metal gem, full of quality song after quality song. Grunge had taken over by the time they released *Ultraphobic* in 1995. Warrant was one of the very few bands that was able to blend the hair metal and grunge genres, at least with one album. "Family Picnic" and "Stronger Now" are fantastic songs.

Warrant Facts:
Originally Based: Hollywood, CA
Formed: 1984
Debut Album Released: 1989

Main band members include:
Erik Turner, Jani Lane, Joey Allen, Jerry Dixon, Steven Sweet, Robert Mason.

Albums: Best, Most Underrated, Last:
Best: *Dog Eat Dog* – 1992
Most Underrated: *Dog Eat Dog* – 1992
Last: *Louder Harder Faster* – 2017

Key Albums:
Dog Eat Dog (#27), *Cherry Pie* (#28), *Dirty Rotten Filthy Stinking Rich* (#41)

Key Songs:
Rock: "Cherry Pie" (#12), "Uncle Tom's Cabin" (#27), "Down Boys" (#47), "Mr. Rainmaker" (#82)
Ballad: "Heaven" (#10), "Stronger Now" (#15), "I Saw Red" (#26), "Sad Theresa" (#45), "Blind Faith" (#68)

Top Songs:
1. "Cherry Pie" – *Cherry Pie*
2. "Uncle Tom's Cabin" – *Cherry Pie*
3. "Down Boys" – *Dirty Rotten Filthy Stinking Rich*
4. "Mr. Rainmaker" – *Cherry Pie*
5. "Thin Disguise" – *Best Of*
6. "Hole In My Wall" – *Dog Eat Dog*
7. "Stronger Now" – *Ultraphobic*
8. "Face" – *Under the Influence*
9. "Heaven" – *Dirty Rotten Filthy Stinking Rich*
10. "Ultraphobic" – *Ultraphobic*
11. "I Saw Red" – *Cherry Pie*
12. "Sad Theresa" – *Dog Eat Dog*
13. "Big Talk" – *Dirty Rotten Filthy Stinking Rich*

14. "Nobody Else" – *Belly To Belly*
15. "Blind Faith" – *Cherry Pie*
16. "Letter to A Friend" – *Belly to Belly*
17. "Bridges are Burning" – *Dog Eat Dog*
18. "Machine Gun" – *Dog Eat Dog*
19. "Family Picnic" – *Ultraphobic*
20. "Sometimes She Cries" – *Dirty Rotten Filthy Stinking Rich*

Top Albums:
1. *Dog Eat Dog* – 1992
2. *Cherry Pie* – 1990
3. *Dirty Rotten Filthy Stinking Rich* – 1989
4. *Ultraphobic* – 1995
5. *Rockaholic* – 2011
6. *Belly to Belly* – 1996

Great White

Led by Jack Russell's smooth voice and the band's blues-rock base, Great White released some of the most pop-friendly rock of the genre.

Great White ended up with three top 25 albums on Billboard and five songs that made the top 60 on the singles chart. They also charted more ballads in our Top 1,000 list than any band of the era, led by "Save Your Love", the genre's fourth best ballad of all time!

Guitar player Mark Kendall and singer Russell actually met and teamed up back in 1977! Their band played a few shows before breaking up when Russell went to prison. Kendall went through a couple different singers before quickly picking Russell back up when the vocal God was released. They hooked up with manager Alan Niven and the rest is history. Their debut EP *Out of the Night* is a classic, showcasing a band that sat closer to the metal side than blues rock band they'd later morph into. One of Great White's first major tours was opening for metal legends Judas Priest.

After the hair metal era started declining, Great White is one of the few bands that still released several very solid albums. Some with Russell on vocals, some without, and Russell with his own version of Great White. You can put on any of GW's 10 best albums and find several good songs on each one.

Great White Facts:
Originally Based: Los Angeles, CA
Formed: 1977

Debut Album Released: 1984

Main band members include:
Mark Kendall, Audie Desbrow, Jack Russell, Michael Lardie, Scott Snyder, Tony Montana.

Albums: Best, Most Underrated, Last:
Best: *Once Bitten* – 1987
Most Underrated: *Sail Away* – 1994
Last: *Full Circle* – 2017

Key Albums:
Once Bitten (#25), *...Twice Shy* (#37), *Sail Away* (#71), *Hooked* (#86)

Key Songs:
Rock: "Rock Me" (#23), "Once Bitten, Twice Shy" (#45), "Lady Red Light" (#71)
Ballad: "Save Your Love" (#4), "Miles Away" (#50), "Silent Night" (#71), "Babe I'm Gonna Leave You" (#78)

Top Songs:
1. "Rock Me" – *Once Bitten*
2. "Save Your Love" – *Once Bitten*
3. "Once Bitten, Twice Shy" – *...Twice Shy*
4. "Lady Red Light" – *Once Bitten*
5. "On Your Knees" – *Out of the Night*
6. "Mista Bone" – *...Twice Shy*
7. "Out of the Night" – *Out of the Night*
8. "Can't Shake It" – *Hooked*
9. "Sail Away" – *Sail Away*
10. "Miles Away" – *Let it Rock*

11. "Desert Moon" – *Hooked*
12. "I Don't Mind" – *Rising*
13. "Silent Night" – *Can't Get There from Here*
14. "Back to the Rhythm" – *Back to the Rhythm*
15. "Afterglow" – *Hooked*
16. "Something for You" – *Elated*
17. "All Over Now" – *Once Bitten*
18. "Rollin' Stoned" – *Can't Get There from Here*
19. "Ain't No Shame" – *Can't Get There from Here*
20. "The Angel Song" – *...Twice Shy*

Top Albums:

1. *Once Bitten* – 1987
2. *...Twice Shy* – 1989
3. *Sail Away* – 1994
4. *Hooked* – 1991
5. *Rising* – 2009
6. *Psycho City* – 1992
7. *Back to the Rhythm* – 2007
8. *Great White* – 1984
9. *Let It Rock* – 1996
10. *Elation* – 2012
11. *Shot in the Dark* – 1986

Dokken

Casual fans don't realize it, but Dokken probably released the first hair metal song of all time with the self–titled track off the 1981 album *Breaking the Chains*.

Dokken had five albums that made the top 50 on Billboard. Their live album *Beast from the East* was nominated for a Grammy in 1989. They put six songs into the top 100 of our HM/HB best songs of all–time list and four albums into the top 100 of our albums of all-time list.

From top–to–bottom, Dokken's classic lineup was one of the most talented bands to come out of the entire genre. Don Dokken on vocals, Jeff Pilson on bass, Mick Brown on the drums and guitar virtuoso George Lynch on guitar. Pilson has great memories of his bandmates, saying this about Don and George:
"(Don) is a great lyricist and can be an extremely generous man" and about Lynch "I don't think people give him the credit he deserves when it comes to songwriting – even melodies and occasionally lyrics. He's way more than just a brilliant guitarist."

After a successful turn overseas but lackluster start in the United States, Dokken was rumored to be close to being dropped by their label. They then re–released *Breakin' the Chains* in 1983, *Tooth and Nail* in 1984 and *Under Lock and Key* in 1985 and they rocketed to being one of the top bands in rock music. Their 1987 release *Back For the Attack* was good enough to land them on the "Monsters of Rock Tour" with Van Halen, Scorpions and Metallica.

Dokken Facts:
Originally Based: Los Angeles, CA
Formed: 1979
Debut Album Released: 1981

Main band members include:
Don Dokken, Mick Brown, George Lynch, Jeff Pilson, John Norum.

Albums: Best, Most Underrated, Last:
Best: *Under Lock and Key* – 1985
Most Underrated: *Lightning Strikes Again* – 2008
Last: *Broken Bones* – 2012

Key Albums:
Tooth and Nail (#18), *Under Lock and Key* (#21), *Breaking the Chains* (#49), *Back for the Attack* (#68)

Key Songs:
Rock: "Breaking the Chains" (#19), "In My Dreams" (#29), "Dream Warriors" (#50), "It's Not Love" (#76),
Ballad: "Alone Again" (#22), "Walk Away" (#33)

Top Songs:
1. "Breaking the Chains" – *Breaking the Chains*
2. "In My Dreams" – *Under Lock and Key*
3. "Dream Warriors" – *Back for the Attack*
4. "It's Not Love" – *Under Lock and Key*
5. "The Hunter" – *Under Lock and Key*
6. "Heaven Sent" – *Back for the Attack*
7. "Alone Again" – *Tooth and Nail*
8. "Paris is Burning" – *Breaking the Chains*
9. "Into the Fire" – *Tooth and Nail*
10. "Tooth and Nail" – *Tooth and Nail*

11. "Just Got Lucky" – *Tooth and Nail*
12. "Walk Away" – *Beast from the East*
13. "Standing on the Outside" – *Lightning Strikes Again*
14. "Goodbye My Friend" – *Long Way Home*
15. "Jaded Heart" – *Under Lock and Key*
16. "Little Girl" – *Long Way Home*
17. "Give Me a Reason" – *Lighting Strikes Again*
18. "Unchain the Night" – *Lock and Key*
19. "The Last Goodbye" – *Hell to Pay*
20. "The Maze" – *Dysfunctional*

Top Albums:
1. *Tooth and Nail* – 1984
2. *Under Lock and Key* – 1985
3. *Breaking the Chains* – 1981
4. *Back for the Attack* – 1987
5. *Beast from the East* – 1988
6. *Lighting Strikes Again* – 2008
7. *Long Way Home* – 2002
8. *Dysfunctional* – 1995
9. *Erase the Slate* – 1999

Ratt

One of the OGs of the genre. Ratt's classic lineup started hitting the Los Angeles circuit in 1981. Just a few short years later the video for "Round and Round" was an MTV staple and Ratt was an A–level band!

Ratt had six albums break the top 40 level on Billboard and five albums land in the top 100 of our Albums list.

"I sometimes say that I hate the term "Rock star" but these days I think rock stars are in short supply. You know, the guys that are a bit larger than life and really live the whole lifestyle? Stephen Pearcy is one of those guys. He's for real and I wish we had more of him," – Danny Vaughn, Tyketto.

The early beginnings of Ratt featured a fun guitar trio. Jake E Lee was in the band but left and recommended 18–year–old college student Warren DiMartini. DiMartini was leery of dropping out of college to join an unknow band, so Marq Torien came and played with Pearcy. Luckily for all involved, DiMartini changed his mind and joined the band. Two years later Ratt was one of the biggest bands in the world.

Ratt, like Dokken, was a step above the majority of hair metal bands to follow simply because of how musically talented the band was. Robbin Crosby and DeMartini were both A–plus guitar players. Juan Croucier was a great bass player and Bobby Blotzer was "The Man" on drums! That lineup, with Pearcy's distinctive vocals, led to a five-year run of albums that helped legitimize the hair metal genre (*Out of the Cellar, Invasion of Your Privacy, Dancing Undercover* and *Reach for the Sky* 1984–1988).

Ratt Facts:
Originally Based: Hollywood, CA
Formed: 1976
Debut Album Released: 1984

Main band members include:
Stephen Pearcy, Juan Croucier, Robbin Crosby, Warren DeMartini, Bobby Blotzer, Robbie Crane, Jizzy Pearl, Carlos Cavazo.

Albums: Best, Most Underrated, Last:
Best: *Out of the Cellar* – 1984
Most Underrated: *Infestation* – 2010
Last: *Infestation* – 2010

Key Albums:
Out of the Cellar (#17), *Invasion of Your Privacy* (#38), *Dancing Undercover* (#43), *Infestation* (#56), *Reach for the Sky* (#72)

Key Songs:
Rock: "Round and Round" (#4), "Lay it Down" (#46), "You're in Love" (#65), "Slip of the Lip" (#68), "I Want a Woman" (#93)
Ballad: "I Want to Love You Tonight" (#70)

Top Songs:
1. "Round and Round" – *Out of the Cellar*
2. "Lay It Down" – *Invasion of Your Privacy*
3. "You're in Love" – *Invasion of Your Privacy*
4. "Slip of the Lip" – *Dancing Undercover*
5. "I Want a Woman" – *Reach for the Sky*

6. "Back for More" – *Out of the Cellar*
7. "Way Cool Jr" – *Reach for the Sky*
8. "Wanted Man" – *Out of the Cellar*
9. "Dance" – *Dancing Undercover*
10. "Best of Me" – *Infestation*
11. "Givin' Yourself Away" – *Detonator*
12. "Lovin' You's a Dirty Job" – *Detonator*
13. "Body Talk" – *Dancing Undercover*
14. "I Want to Love You Tonight' – *Reach for the Sky*
15. "As Good as It Gets" – *Infestation*

Top Albums:
1. *Out of the Cellar* – 1984
2. *Invasion of Your Privacy* – 1985
3. *Dancing Undercover* – 1986
4. *Infestation* – 2010
5. *Reach for the Sky* – 1988
6. *Detonator* – 1990
7. *Ratt* – 1999

Poison

One of the most popular pure "hair bands" of the entire era. Makeup, spandex, cheesy lyrics...and the band didn't apologize for any of it. And female fans couldn't get enough!

Poison was one of the most commercially successful bands of the genre. They scored eight top 20 songs on Billboard, including three that made the top five. They also sold more than 40 million albums, which, depending on whose "numbers" you believe would make them fifth highest selling band of the genre. Three of their albums cracked the top 10 on Billboard 200. Power ballad "Every Rose Has its Thorn" went all the way to number one.

Poison placed three albums in our top 350 Albums of all-time chart.

"I believe the answer lies in how hard you work at it, and not really in your level of talent. Poison worked and worked and worked every day and every night, promoting themselves like mad. They were an inspiration to all Sunset bands. Brett was on the strip 24/7 it seems, chit-chatting everybody about Poison. CC is an excellent bluesy player in my book, as I caught him in coffee shops and dive bars in Hollywood quite a few times in the 90's. And Brett is so fucking good looking, does it matter that he doesn't really sing like Ronnie James Dio?" – Pat Fontaine, XYZ.

Poison Facts:
Originally Based: Mechanicsburg, PA
Formed: 1983
Debut Album Released: 1986

Main band members include:
C.C. DeVille, Bobby Dall, Rikki Rockett, Bret Michaels.

Albums: Best, Most Underrated, Last
Best: *Open Up and Say...Ahh!* – 1988
Most Underrated: *Flesh & Blood* – 1990
Last: *Poison'd* – 2007

Key Albums:
Open Up and Say...Ahh! (#16), *Look What the Cat Dragged In* (#35), *Flesh & Blood* (#48)

Key Songs:
Rock: "Nothin' But A Good Time" (#30), "Talk Dirty to Me" (#32),
Ballad: "Every Rose Has its Thorn" (#20), "Something to Believe In" (#48), "I Won't Forget You" (#65), "Life Goes On" (#67)

Top Songs:
1. "Nothin' but a Good Time" – *Open Up and Say...Ahh!*
2. "Talk Dirty to Me" – *Look What the Cat Dragged In*
3. "Fallen Angel" – *Open Up and Say...Ahh!*
4. "Every Rose Has Its Thorn" – *Open Up and Say...Ahh!*
5. "Ride the Wind" – *Flesh & Blood*
6. "Something to Believe In" – *Flesh & Blood*
7. "Unskinny Bop" – *Flesh & Blood*
8. "I Won't Forget You" – *Look What the Cat Dragged In*
9. "Stand" – *Native Tongue*
10. "Life Goes On" – *Flesh & Blood*
11. "Only Time Will Tell" – *Swallow This Live*
12. "Stand" – *Native Tongue*

13. "Look What the Cat Dragged in" – *Look What the Cat Dragged In*
14. "So Tell Me Why" – *Swallow This Live*
15. "I Want Action" – *Look What the Cat Dragged In*

Top Albums:
1. *Open Up and Say...Ahh!* – 1988
2. *Look What the Cat Dragged In* – 1986
3. *Flesh & Blood* – 1990
4. *Native Tongue* – 1993
5. *Crack a Smile...and More* – 2000

KIX

East coast legends led by the vocal mastery of Steve Whiteman.

KIX had released three fairly well reviewed albums before softening their sound up just a bit and striking gold with their 1988 release *Blow My Fuse*, which came in as our 14th best album of all time. The songs "Cold Blood" and "Don't Close Your Eyes" both finished as top 16 songs on our top songs list.

Along with several quality albums, KIX also makes the Hall of Fame based on their incredible live shows. They were – and still are – one of the best live bands of the entire genre. The band is also extremely respected amongst other musicians as being one of the friendliest and classiest bands around.

"KIX is a must (see)! Love Steve Whiteman, that guy is incredible," – Anthony Corder, Tora Tora.

Kix Facts:
Originally Based: Hagerstown, MD
Formed: 1977
Debut Album Released: 1981

Main Band Members include:
Brian Forsythe, Ronnie Younkins, Steve Whiteman, Jimmy Chalfant, Donnie Purnell, Mark Schenker.

Albums: Best, Most Underrated, Last
Best: *Blow My Fuse* – 1988
Most Underrated: *Rock Your Face Off* – 2014

Last: *Rock Your Face Off* – 2014

Key Albums:
Blow My Fuse (#14), *Midnite Dynamite* (#91), *Hot Wire* (#121)

Key Songs:
Rock: "Cold Blood" (#16), "Blow My Fuse" (#122), "You're Gone" (#258)
Ballad: "Don't Close Your Eyes" (#12), "For Shame" (#51), "Tear Down the Walls" (#132)

Top Songs:
1. "Cold Blood" – *Blow My Fuse*
2. "Don't Close Your Eyes" – *Blow My Fuse*
3. "Blow My Fuse" – *Blow My Fuse*
4. "For Shame" – *Cool Kids*
5. "Tear Down the Walls" – *Hot Wire*
6. "Inside Outside Inn" – *Rock Your Face Off*
7. "You're Gone" – *Rock Your Face Off*
8. "Walkin' Away" – *Midnite Dynamite*
9. "If You Run Around" – *Show Business*
10. "Cold Shower" – *Midnite Dynamite*

Top Albums:
1. *Blow My Fuse* – 1988
2. *Midnite Dynamite* – 1995
3. *Hot Wire* – 1991
4. *Rock Your Face Off* – 2014
5. *Show Business* – 1995
6. *Cool Kids* – 1983

Cinderella

Cinderella is another group that was a hard rock band at heart but got lumped into the HM/HB territory just based on the time period they broke into the scene. With Tom Keifer's gravely vocals and the band's blues–rock sound, Cinderella was one of the more unique sounding bands of the era.

Cinderella ended up with three of their four albums cracking the top 20 album chart on Billboard. They had five songs make the Billboard top 40. Cinderella released some of the finest power ballads of the era. Three placed within the top 25 on our Ballads chart.

"(Fred Coury) is the nicest, happiest guy I have ever met. It is fun to hang with him. All the guys in that camp are cool and Tom is a very talented singer/writer." – Joey Allen, Warrant.

Cinderella is also unique in that they only released four albums, three during the hair metal heyday. But what great albums they were. *Night Songs*, *Long Cold Winter*, and *Heartbreak Station* are considered rock classics. Those three all finished in the top 35 of our all-time album list.

Cinderella Facts:
Originally Based: Philadelphia, PA
Formed: 1982
Debut Album Released: 1986

Main band members include:
Tom Keifer, Eric Brittingham, Jeff LaBar, Fred Coury, Gary Corbett.

Albums: Best, Most Underrated, Last
Best: *Night* Songs – 1986
Most Underrated: *Heartbreak Station* – 1990
Last: *Still Climbing* – 1994

Key Albums:
Long Cold Winter (#11), *Night Songs* (#12), *Heartbreak Station* (#34), *Still Climbing* (#125)

Key Songs:
Rock: "Shake Me" (#31), "Gypsy Road" (#35), "Shelter Me" (#58), "Somebody Save Me" (#64)
Ballad: "Don't Know What You've Got" (#5), "Coming Home" (#14), "Nobody's Fool" (#23), "Heartbreak Station" (#73), "Long Cold Winter" (#82)

Top Songs:
1. "Gypsy Road " – *Long Cold Winter*
2. "Don't Know What You Got" – *Long Cold Winter*
3. "Shake Me" – *Night Songs*
4. "Coming Home" – *Long Cold Winter*
5. "Shelter Me" – *Heartbreak Station*
6. "Nobody's Fool" – *Night Songs*
7. "Somebody Save Me" – *Night Songs*
8. "Heartbreak Station" – *Heartbreak Station*
9. "Bad Seamstress Blues" – *Long Cold Winter*
10. "Long Cold Winter" – *Long Cold Winter*
11. "Night Songs" – *Night Songs*
12. "Through the Rain" – *Still Climbing*
13. "Last Mile" – *Long Cold Winter*
14. "Bad Attitude Shuffle" – *Still Climbing*
15. "Hard to Find the Words" – *Still Climbing*

Openers

Every tour needs a solid opener. A band that can pull in some audience and will put on a great show. These are bands that the Big Boys want to bring on tour with them.

Some of them had a couple minor hits, or one great album, or they have an iconic member. Very solid bands that just missed out being headliners. The bands with Gold records instead of Platinum ones.

These guys are on the opening floor of the Hall of Fame.

Mr. Big

Mr. Big might have had the most talented collection of musicians of any of the bands that played in the HM/HB genre. Eric Martin has the golden voice, Paul Gilbert is a Guitar God, Billy Sheehan is probably the best bass player of the entire genre, and Pat Torpey was a master behind the kit.

Mr. Big had one of the last number one hit songs of the genre, hitting the Billboard top spot with "To Be With You" back in 1992.

Here is what Sheehan had to say about his band members:

Gilbert: "Dear friend, brilliant player."
Torpey: "Also like a brother to me, supreme grand master of drums, incredible singer, and dearly missed every single day."

Martin: "A voice as good as it gets, brilliant songwriter, very dear friend."

Mr. Big Facts
Originally Based: Los Angeles, CA
Formed: 1988
Debut Album Released: 1989

Main band members include:
Eric Martin, Billy Sheehan, Paul Gilbert, Pat Torpey.

Key Albums:
Lean Into It (#82), *Mr. Big* (#160)

Key Songs:
Ballad: "To Be With You" (#19), "Wild World" (#75), "Anything For You" (#93)

Top Songs:
1. "To Be With You" – *Lean Into It*
2. "Green–Tinted Sixties Mind" – *Lean Into It*
3. "If That's What It Takes" – *Hey Man*
4. "Addicted to That Rush" – *Mr. Big*
5. "Lost in America" – *Actual Size*
6. "Anything for You" – *Mr. Big*
7. "Undertow" – *What If...*
8. "Little Mistake" – *Hey Man*
9. "Gotta Love the Ride" – *...The Stories We Could Tell*
10. "Just Take My Heart When You Go" – *Lean Into It*

Top Albums:
1. *Mr. Big* – 1989
2. *Lean Into It* – 1991
3. *Actual Size* – 2001

4. *Hey Man* – 1996
5. *…The Stories We Could* Tell – 2014
6. *Bump Ahead* – 1993
7. *What If…* – 2011

White Lion

A great singer and underrated songwriter in Mike Tramp, plus a Guitar God in Vito Bratta made White Lion one of the most recognizable bands of the era. Like Warrant, White Lion was known for their ballads and more pop–rock hits, but on stage the WL boys were a much heavier band.

We listed three White Lion albums in our top 100 albums of all-time list. The songs "Wait" and "When the Children Cry" both made the top 10 on the Billboard singles chart.

White Lion Facts
Originally Based: New York, NY
Formed: 1983
Debut Album Released: 1985

Main Band Members:
Mike Tramp, Vito Bratta, James LoMenzo, Greg D'Angelo. Jamie Law, Troy Patrick Farrell, Claus Langeskov and Henning Wanner all played for the band between 2004–2013.

Key Songs:
Rock: "Wait" (#54), "Broken Heart" (#63)
Ballads: "When the Children Cry" (#74)

Key Albums:
Big Game (#52), *Pride* (#51), *Mane Attraction* (#98)

Top Songs:
1. "Wait" – "Pride"
2. "Broken Heart" – *Fight to Survive*
3. "Little Fighter" – *Big Game*
4. "When the Children Cry" – *Pride*
5. "Tell Me" – *Pride*
6. "Radar Love" – *Big Game*
7. "Out With the Boys" – *Main Attraction*
8. "You're All I Need" – *Main Attraction*
9. "Love Don't Come Easy" – *Main Attraction*
10. "Dream" – *Return of the Pride*

Top Albums:
1. *Big Game* – 1989
2. *Pride* – 1987
3. *Mane Attraction* – 1991
4. *Return of the Pride* – 2008

Winger

Another great band full of All-Star level musicians, led by the singer–guitar player duo of Kip Winger and Reb Beach. Throw in hall of fame level drummer Rob Morgenstein and jack–of–all–trades Paul Taylor and it's still a mystery why Winger wasn't as huge as Bon Jovi and Def Leppard.

Key Music: "Headed for a Heartbreak", "Seventeen" and the self–titled album *Winger*.

Winger Facts:
Originally Based: New York, NY
Formed: 1987
Debut Album Released: 1988

Main Band Members:
Kip Winger, Reb Beach, Rod Morgenstein, Paul Taylor, John Roth.

Top Songs:
1. "Seventeen" – *Winger*
2. "Hungry" – *Winger*
3. "Headed for a Heartbreak" – *Winger*
4. "Easy Come Easy Go" – *In the Heart of the Young*
5. "Without the Night" – *Winger*
6. "Can't Get Enuff" – *In the Heart of the Young*
7. "Big World Away" – *Karma*
8. "Miles Away" – *In the Heart of the Young*
9. "After All This Time" – *Karma*
10. "Out of This World" – *Better Days Comin'*

Top Albums:
1. *Winger* – 1988
2. *In the Heart of the Young* – 1990
3. *IV* – 2006
4. *Karma* – 2009
5. *Better Days Comin'* – 2014
6. *Pull* – 1993

FireHouse

Great pop–rock band...a poor man's Bon Jovi.

FireHouse was known for their strong heart–wrenching ballads. They had four songs make the Billboard top 30, and two albums crack the top 25 on the album chart.

Based on their incredible debut album, FireHouse beat out Nirvana and Alice in Chains for the award "Favorite Heavy Metal/Hard Rock New Artist" at the 1992 American Music Awards.

Key Music: "Love of a Lifetime" and "Don't Treat Me Bad".

FireHouse Facts
Originally Based: Richmond, VA
Formed: 1989
Debut Album Released: 1990

Main Band Members:
C.J. Snare, Bill Leverty, Michael Foster, Perry Richardson, Allen McKenzie.

Top Songs:
1. "Don't Treat Me Bad" – *FireHouse*
2. "Shake & Tumble" – *FireHouse*
3. "All She Wrote" – *FireHouse*
4. "Love of a Lifetime" – *FireHouse*
5. "Reach for the Sky" – *Hold Your Fire*
6. "When I Look into Your Eyes" – *Hold Your Fire*
7. "Bringing me Down" – *Category 5*
8. "Hold the Dream" – *Hold Your Fire*
9. "Love Is a Dangerous Thing" – *3*
10. "I Live My Life for You" – *3*

Top Albums:
1. *FireHouse* – 1990

2. *Hold Your Fire* – 1992
3. *3* – 1995
4. *Category 5* – 1998
5. *Full Circle* – 2011

Slaughter

Led by amazing vocalist Mark Slaughter, Slaughter had two Billboard top 20 albums and two of the more iconic songs of the genre!

We've got "Up All Night" as the 25th best rock song and "Fly to the Angels" as the 30th best power ballad.

Slaughter and bass player Dana Strum were originally in the Vinnie Vincent Invasion. The label got frustrated with Vinnie and gave the band's contract over to Slaughter and Strum who promptly hired Tim Kelly and Blas Elias and then went on to release two consecutive platinum albums!

Slaughter Facts:
Originally Based: Las Vegas, NV
Formed: 1988
Debut Album Released: 1990

Main Band Members:
Mark Slaughter, Dana Strum, Jeff Bland, Tim Kelly, Blas Elias.

Key Music: "Up All Night" and "Fly to the Angels". Two great albums in *Stick it to Ya* and *The Wild Life*.

Top Songs:
1. "Up All Night" – *Stick It to Ya*
2. "Mad About You" – *Stick It to Ya*
3. "Fly To The Angels" – *Stick It to Ya*
4. "Searchin'" – *Fear No Evil*
5. "Real Love" – *The Wild Life*
6. "Spend My Life" – *Stick It to Ya*
7. "Days Gone Bye" – *The Wild Life*
8. "You're My Everything" – *Revolution*
9. "Wild Life" – *The Wild Life*
10. "Hard To Say Goodbye" – *Slaughter*

Top Albums:
1. *Stick It to Ya* – 1990
2. *The Wild Life* – 1992
3. *Fear No Evil* – 1995
4. *Revolution* – 1997
5. *Back to Reality* – 1999

Stryper

A band that doesn't get the credit they deserve from most rock fans. The Christian rockers released five albums that landed in the top 50 on Billboard.

Stryper was most known for their outstanding vocalist Michael Sweet, and for being one of the rare Christian metal bands to break big.

For whatever reason, Stryper is extremely popular overseas. Outselling bands like Motley Crue and Bon Jovi in some countries.

Drummer Tim Gaines on his former band's success:

"It was a combination of our look, sounds, and message. Different people liked different things about us. Some hated our message but loved the songs, while others loved the message, and finally found a band they could listen to with a positive message and good music."

Stryper Facts:
Originally Based: Orange County, CA
Formed: 1983
Debut Album Released: 1984

Main Band Members:
Michael Sweet, Robert Sweet, Oz Fox, Tim Gaines

Key Music: "Honestly" and the album *In God We Trust*.

Top Songs:
1. "Honestly" – *To Hell With The Devil*
2. "No More Hell to Pay" – *No More Hell To Pay*
3. "In God We Trust" – *In God We Trust*
4. "Against the Law" – *Against the Law*
5. "All Over Again" – *Fallen*
6. "To Hell With The Devil" – *To Hell With The Devil*
7. "My Love" – *Murder By Pride*
8. "You Won't Be Lonely" – *The Yellow and Black Attack*
9. "Fallen" – *Fallen*
10. "Soldiers Under Command" – *Soldiers Under Command*

Top Albums:
1. *In God We Trust* – 1988
2. *Against the Law* – 1990
3. *To Hell with The Devil* – 1986
4. *No More Hell to Pay* – 2013
5. *Fallen* – 2015
6. *The Yellow and Black Attack* – 1984

Vixen

The most successful female group of the genre! Vixen joins the Hall mainly based on their amazing 1988 self-titled album, along with being a fantastic live band.

The album *Vixen* not only produced two top 20 hits on Billboard – "Edge of a Broken Heart" and "Cryin" but Rolling Stone magazine named it as the 43 best hair metal album in history.

Vixen is still currently touring but is now being fronted by the mega-talented Lorraine Lewis, who you may know from the band Femme Fatale.

Vixen Facts:
Originally Based: St. Paul, MN
Formed: 1980
Debut Album Released: 1988

Main Band Members:
Janet Gardner, Roxy Petrucci, Share Ross, Chris Fayz, Jan Kuehnemund, Lorraine Lewis.

Key Music: "Edge of a Broken Heart", "Cryin", "How Much Love".

Top Songs:
1. "Edge of a Broken Heart" – *Vixen*
2. "Cryin" – *Vixen*
3. "How Much Love" – *Rev it Up*
4. "Love Made Me" – *Vixen*
5. "Love is a Killer" – *Rev it Up*
6. "Not a Minute Too Soon" – *Rev it Up*
7. "Page" – *Tangerine*

Top Albums:
1. *Vixen* – 1988
2. *Rev It Up* – 1990

Europe

Known for two hit songs (both top 10 on Billboard) and two hit albums (both top 20 on Billboard), Europe has continued to release strong albums over the last two decades.

The band's 2000s albums stack up against almost anybody else's in the genre.

"The Final Countdown" is a hair metal staple, as is the power ballad "Carrie".

Europe Facts:
Originally Based: Upplands Vasby, Sweden
Formed: 1979
Debut Album Released: 1983

Key Music: "The Final Countdown" and "Carrie".

Top Songs:
1. "The Final Countdown" – The Final Countdown
2. "Rock the Night" – The Final Countdown
3. "Carrie" – The Final Countdown
4. "Bag of Bones" – Bag of Bones
5. "Gonna Get Ready" – Last Look at Eden
6. "Superstitious" – Out of this World
7. "New Love in Town" – Last Look at Eden
8. "Last Look at Eden" – Last Look at Eden
9. "Always the Pretender" – Secret Society
10. "Praise You" – War of Kings

Top Albums:
1. *The Final Countdown* – 1986
2. *Out of This World* – 1988
3. *Last Look at Eden* – 2009
4. *Start from The Dark* – 2004
5. *Bag of Bones* – 2012

THE GODFATHERS

These three bands broke into the scene early and greatly influenced all the bands that followed. Two of the bands had a couple major albums and hits…while one didn't reach super stardom, but their sound/style clearly influenced numerous of the popular bands that followed.

Quiet Riot

One of the bands that helped kick start the entire hair metal genre! The album *Metal Health* went to #1 on Billboard in 1983 and was the first "metal" album to ever top the charts. "Cum on Feel the Noize" is a genre classic.

The original Quiet Riot featured rock legend Randy Rhoads on guitar and vocalist Kevin DuBrow, both who have passed away. That version of the band recorded two albums that were only released in Japan. Rhoads and bass player Rudy Sarzo left QR to play for Ozzy Osbourne, while DuBrow chose to retire the Quiet Riot name and started performing as DuBrow.

Luckily, a couple years later DuBrow put a really solid band together and decided to reignite the Quiet Riot name. A year later they released *Metal Health* and history was made.

QR released three albums between 1983–1986 that cracked the Billboard top 40 album charts. We ranked "Cum on Feel the Noize" as the third best overall song of the genre (right behind "Welcome to the Jungle" and "Photograph") and

"Metal Health" as the 26th best song. We've ranked the album *Metal Health* as the 20th best album of all time.

Quiet Riot Facts:
Originally Based: Los Angeles, CA
Formed: 1973
Debut Album Released: 1977 (Japan) and 1983 (United States).

Main Band Members:
Kevin DuBrow, Frankie Banali, Chuck Wright, Alex Grossi, Randy Rhoads, Rudy Sarzo, Carlos Cavazo.

Key Music: *Metal Health* the album and song, and the song "Cum on Feel the Noize".

Top Songs:
1. "Cum On Feel the Noize" – *Metal Health*
2. "Metal Health" – *Metal Health*
3. "Mama Weer All Crazee Now" – *Condition Critical*
4. "Down to the Bone" – *Down to the Bone*
5. "Stay with Me Tonight" – *Quiet Riot I*
6. "The Wild and the Young" – *Quiet Riot III*
7. "Thunderbird" – *Metal Health*
8. "Slick Black Cadillac" – *Quiet Riot II*
9. "Let's Get Crazy" – *Metal Health*
10. "Callin' the Shots" – *Quiet Riot*

Top Albums:
1. *Metal Health* - 1983
2. *Condition Critical* - 1984
3. *Down to the Bone* - 1995
4. *QR* - 1988
5. *Quiet Riot II*

Twisted Sister

Dee Snider's look, singing and fight against Tipper Gore would be enough to earn him a spot in the Hall of Fame. If that wasn't enough, his band Twisted Sister is one of the greatest live bands of all time.

Don't be fooled by the big hair and makeup. In their prime Twisted Sister kicked a lot of ass. In the early days Twisted toured with bands like Metallica and Motorhead. They started off in the early 70s and spent a solid decade grinding it out, playing live club shows on a nightly basis. Breakthrough commercial success came in 1984 with the release of *Stay Hungry*, which went triple platinum. *Stay Hungry* also produced the band's two biggest Billboard and MTV hits: "We're Not Gonna Take It" and "I Wanna Rock".

Twisted Sister are also generally regarded as one of the best live bands of the last 50 years. And if that wasn't enough, the band also released a Christmas album in 2006 that received stellar reviews.

"We never really dealt with Twisted Sister because they just turned up and played and then left. But fuck they were loud. I know most bands say they're loud but other than Motörhead, Sister was the only band I've ever seen that I really noticed how loud they actually were. I loved them though!" – Kim Hooker, Tigertailz

"We come to every show with the purpose of demolishing and demoralizing the competition. This is not a Kumbaya way to engender a 'family spirit' but it does lead to a night of great entertainment for the fans which, at the end of the day, is all that really matters. Seeing us live has been called a "religious experience" by too many journalists (and fans) who witness our power." – Jay Jay French, Twisted Sister

Twisted Sister Facts:
Originally Based: Ho-Ho-Kus, NJ
Formed: 1972
Debut Album Released: 1982

Main Band Members:
Dee Snider – vocals
Jay Jay French – guitar
Eddie Ojeda – guitar
Mark Mendoza – bass
A.J. Pero – drums

Top Songs:
1. "We're Not Gonna Take It" – *Stay Hungry*
2. "You Can't Stop Rock 'n' Roll" – *You Can't Stop Rock 'n' Roll*
3. "I Wanna Rock" – *Stay Hungry*
4. "You're Not Alone" – *You Can't Stop Rock 'n' Roll*
5. "The Price" – *Stay Hungry*
6. "Bad Boys" – *Under the Blade*
7. "I Believe In You" – *Come Out and Play*
8. "Under the Blade" – *Under the Blade*
9. "I Am (I'm Me)" – *You Can't Stop Rock 'n' Roll*
10. "Tear it Loose" – *Under the Blade*

Top Albums:
1. *You Can't Stop Rock n Roll* – 1983
2. *Stay Hungry* – 1984
3. *Under the Blade* – 1982
4. *Come Out and Play* – 1985

Hanoi Rocks

Michael Monroe and Hanoi Rocks were a fascinating band. They didn't have a huge breakout album or song, but dozens upon dozens of major rock superstars list Hanoi Rocks as being major influences. Members of Guns N' Roses and Def Leppard talk about how awesome and influential Hanoi was.

There were really two eras of the band. Hanoi, originally from Finland, started off in 1979 and were really considered rising superstars as they were popular around the world – from the UK all the way to Japan! But exciting drummer Nicholas "Razzle" Dingley was killed in a drunk driving accident. The tragic loss of Razzle was too much to overcome and the band broke up for almost twenty years.

Monroe and guitar player Andy McCoy brought the band back together for almost a decade, reforming in 2001 and lasting through 2009.

Hanoi Rocks Facts:
Originally Based: Helsinki, Finland
Formed: 1979
Debut Album Released: 1981

Main Band Members:
Michael Monroe – vocals
Nasty Suicide – guitar
Andy McCoy – guitar
Sami Yaffa – bass
Razzle – drums
Lacu – drums
Conny Bloom – guitar

Andy Christell – bass

Top Songs:
1. "Boulevard of Broken Dreams" – *Two Steps from the Move*
2. "Don't You Ever Leave Me" – *Two Steps from the Move*
3. "Fashion" – *Street Poetry*
4. "A Day Late, A Dollar Short" – *Twelve Shots on the Rocks*
5. "In My Darkest Moment" – *Twelve Shots On the Rocks*
6. "Teenage Revolution" – *Street Poetry*
7. "Two Steps from the Move" – *Two Steps from the Move*
8. "Malibu Beach Nightmare" – *Back to Mystery City*
9. "Million Miles Away" – *Two Steps from the Move*
10. "Until I Get You" – *Back to Mystery City*

Top Albums:
1. *Two Steps from the Move* – 1984
2. *Twelve Shots On the Rocks* – 2002
3. *Street Poetry* – 2007
4. *Back to Mystery City* – 1983

Individual Hall of Fame

Who is the top Hair Metal musician of all time? That's a hard one to choose...but we stepped up to the plate and met the challenge. The genre has so many superstars, iconic figures and larger than life characters, that coming up with a #1 choice took weeks of interviews, debates and near fist–fights. We searched through all the usual candidates and weighed their pluses and minuses to come up with our top choice as the Ultimate Hair Metal Hero!

Our number one choice had to be multi–talented. They couldn't just be amazing at one aspect of being in a band. If you were a great singer, but didn't write your songs or play an instrument, then you didn't advance to the final rounds. Being an iconic figure also counted. As well as how you performed live. And how beloved and respected you were by fans and by critics.

Below is our list for the Ultimate Hair Metal musicians. The most iconic figures of the entire genre.

Winning the coveted position as the Greatest Hair Metal Rocker of All Time:

Jani Lane – The GOAT

Vocals: Lane fit into that great middle groove of vocals that seemed to please all fans. Guys like Axl Rose and Tom Keifer are incredible singers, but they have voices that people either love or hate. Lane had that voice that everybody enjoyed. He could sing the harder type songs, the more pop orientated music, and he absolutely nailed the power ballads.

"He truly was such a great talent. His lyrics, voice and music is timeless. Especially the ballads," – Kristy Majors, Pretty Boy Floyd.

Songwriting: Many people consider Lane and GnR's Izzy Stradlin to be the best songwriters of the genre.

"I did several runs with Jani, mainly doing the Warrant set. He was hands down one of the best songwriters of the genre. It came so naturally to him, he was very gifted – and also funny as hell," – Alex Grossi, Quiet Riot and Hookers & Blow.

"Jani was a great writer. I wish he had gotten more credit for that," – Paul Laine, Danger Danger and The Defiants.

Iconic factor:

"He was a very cool guy at that time (when the two bands toured together). Certainly, he was nice to us and I absolutely never heard a bad word from a fan about him when we were touring," – Ted Poley, Danger Danger.

"One thing I found truly amazing about Jani, he could smoke, drink and party all night, and he would be able to get on stage and sing and perform like a true pro, every night! Never complain, never worried, just got up there and kicked their ass every night! It was truly supernatural and amazing to see. He was very kind, generous and certainly loved to lead the party!" – Mark Gus Scott, Trixter

And isn't "Cherry Pie" the greatest strip club song in history? That's a pretty iconic song!!!

Live / Front Man: Anybody who was a fan of Warrant and saw the band in concert tell you that Lane was one of the best live singers/performers of the genre. Warrant were much heavier live than a lot of people realize.

"Jani was literally a Quiet Riot. Fun to be around but I could always tell he was inside his own head a lot and struggled. He was a brother though and we had some epic times together. Very competitive, very talented and underrated in a big way! One of the best front men in that era as well," – PJ Farley, Trixter.

"A lot of people look at Jani as an '80s hair metal guy, but he was so much deeper than that. I did a lot of shows with Jani and Warrant, and there is no doubt in my mind that he loved this business more than anyone I've ever met, and nobody ever worked as hard onstage as Jani. Maybe James Brown, but I can think of no one else," – singer Joey C. Jones

Instruments: Lane was efficient on several instruments.

"One of the most well–rounded musicians from a very non-musical era. A lot of people don't know that Jani was more than a singer-songwriter. He was an excellent guitar player, bass player, drummer, piano player, and he recorded some songs with producer Dito Godwin, who did the Joey C. Jones and the Gloryhounds album, and I feel that those songs were Jani's best work. I don't know why that stuff has not been released – I guess Dito Godwin is holding onto it – but this stuff is just fantastic." – singer Joey C. Jones

Songs: Warrant was definitely in the upper echelon in terms of the amount of quality music they produced. *Dog Eat Dog* was an underrated masterpiece. Songs like "Down Boys", "Uncle Tom's Cabin", "Cherry Pie", "Heaven", "Sometimes She's Cries", "I Saw Red" and "Blind Faith" will live on in hair metal eternity.

Joining Lane in our individual Hall of Fame:

Slash
Iconic guitar player for Guns N' Roses, Velvet Revolver, and Slash and the Conspirators.

"Well, he's amazing. Pure and simple. I learned A LOT from working with him." – Tony Montana, Great White

"Slash is a legend plain and simple. A rock icon, but unbelievably chill. Incredibly humble and down to earth, I honestly couldn't believe how kind he was on a day-to-day basis. He gave us notes on our set, he told us stories, he was unreal. You learn something from everyone but the secrets I learned from Slash I ain't telling anyone." Max Perenchio, Bad City

Warren DiMartini
Guitar God from legendary band Ratt.

"Riff and melodic legend." – Jay Pepper, Tigertailz

"Warren DiMartini," Beau Nasty's Brian Young when asked who was the best hair metal guitar player.

"He's one of the best in the business and the nicest guy you could meet," – Joey Allen, Warrant.

Billy Sheehan
Sheehan is one of the most famous bass players in music history. Famous from Mr. Big, Talas, Winery Dogs, and Sons of Apollo.

"The best soloing bassist alive. And the reason is that he comes from deep roots that involve grooving and soul, which makes his soloing so special and musical," – legendary Dokken bass player Jeff Pilson.

Rod Morgenstein
Ultra-talented drummer from Winger. Rolling Stone magazine listed Rod as one of the twenty best drummers in history – in ALL music history, not just metal.

Axl Rose
According to one report, Axl has the greatest vocal range of any recorded singer in rock history! Guns N' Roses changed the sound of rock music.

Vito Bratta
A true guitar master. White Lion's Vito showed that a memorable solo wasn't just about speed and shredding, but about melody and doing things nobody else was doing. His solo in Wait was enough to make the Hall of Fame.

Rudy Sarzo
Bass player with an unmatched resume: Quiet Riot, Whitesnake, Ozzy, Dio, Blue Oyster Cult, and Queensryche.

Mark Mendoza
The Monster became famous for his killer bass work for the legendary Twisted Sister.

Tommy Lee
Motley Crue's madman on the kit is known for being a rock-n-roll hero, but he's actually an extremely skilled artist.

Don Dokken
Dokken released the first ever official hair metal album! Don is considered one of the first true hair metal stars. Magical voice and is basically an "uncle" to an entire generation of singers.

George Lynch
Dokken and Lynch Mob axe-man.

"Love to listen to George. I remember painting fences while listening to *Under Lock and Key*...his phrasing is killer and totally original," – Warrant's Joey Allen.

Paul Gilbert
One of the most creative and innovative guitar players in the world. Gained stardom from his time with Mr. Big.

Jimmy D'Anda
Marq Torien gets the glory, but many feel that drummer Jimmy was the heart and soul of The BulletBoys.

Akira Takasaki
Shredding guitar master from the Japanese band Loudness.

Blas Elias
Famous for drumming in the band Slaughter. Did you know Blas also performs with The Blue Man Group and The Trans–Siberian Orchestra?

Vik Foxx
Pounded the kit for Enuff Z'Nuff and the Vince Neil solo band.

Steve Lynch
Underrated guitar player from Autograph. Brought tapping to the rock world before Eddie Van Halen did.

Greg Chaisson
Badlands bassist who does it all: plays incredible bass, sings, writes, produces.

Jack Russell
Most known for fronting Great White and often compared to Led Zeppelin's legendary Robert Plant.

David Coverdale
The Godfather of the genre. Coverdale earns this spot for his band Whitesnake.

Reb Beach
Amazing guitar player for Winger and Whitesnake.

Jeff Pilson
Multi-talented bass player most known for his work with Dokken. Also played with Dio and Foreigner.

Sebastian Bach
The former voice of Skid Row, Bach possessed not only one of the best genre voices, but one of the most powerful voices of the entire rock world.

Frankie Banali
Most known from his drumming with Quiet Riot. Frankie also played with WASP.

Eric Martin
Mr. Big's lead singer once dubbed as having the best voice in rock music.

Joe Elliott
Lead singer for Def Leppard, who were recently inducted in the actual Rock & Roll Hall of Fame.

Tom Keifer
Tom possesses one of the most unique and well-known voices of the genre. He's also a standout guitar player and has released a couple really strong solo albums.

Robert Sweet
The drummer started the band Stryper with his brother Michael. Robert is known as one of the best time-keepers in the business.

A.J. Pero
Superstar drummer earned his stripes with Twisted Sister.

Richie Kotzen
Guitar player for Poison, Mr. Big, and Winery Dogs and has been featured on more than 50 albums. Prolific solo artist.

Juan Croucier
Bass player with the best stage moves. He tore it up with Quiet Riot, Dokken and Ratt.

Ronni Le Tekro
One of the original Guitar Gods...became famous with TnT.

Kyle Kyle
Original bass player and founding member for the underrated Bang Tango.

Pepsi Tate
Founding member and bass player for Tigertailz.

Mick Brown
Drummer Brown is the only member other than Don that has appeared on every Dokken album. Mick also played with Lynch Mob and Ted Nugent.

Fred Coury
The Cinderella drummer is such a beast that he has filled in for Ozzy and Guns N' Roses when their drummers were ill. He also played in the criminally underrated Arcade with Stephen Pearcy.

Stephen Pearcy
The Ratt founder and singer has one of the most distinctive voices in rock music.

Rick Savage
Founding member of Def Leppard back in 1977 and been with the band ever since. One of the most solid bass players in the business.

Dee Snider
One of the original metal giants, the lead singer of Twisted Sister also earned a spot on this list because of his court battles with Tipper Gore and the PMRC.

Jesper Binzer
D.A.D. singer Binzer's band barely fell into the hair metal category. They were good enough to be stalwarts in any genre, in any time period.

Nikki Sixx
Makes the Hall for being one of the most iconic members of the genre. Chief writer and promoter, as well as the face of Motley Crue.

Rachel Bolan
Bassist and main songwriter for Skid Row.

Lita Ford
The most familiar female face of the genre. Great singer, fantastic guitar player.

Stevie Rachelle
Rachelle is the Swiss Army Knife of the genre. Famous for fronting Tuff, Shameless, Cheeseheads with Attitude, Tales From the Porn, created the infamous Metal Sludge website, and managed Vains of Jenna. One of the most astute businessmen and hard-working artists in rock music.

CHECK OUT OUR OTHER METAL BOOKS!
ALL AVAILABLE ON AMAZON

Soundtrack of our Youth – History of Hair Metal Music

Demos & B-Sides

HEAVY METAL AND ROCK ACTIVITY BOOKS: TRIVIA, CROSSWORD PUZZLES, WORD PUZZLES – AVAILABLE ON AMAZON

Printed in Great Britain
by Amazon